INVISIBLE TO

PREDATORS

To Lynn
With all of
my love, BB

Yours,
RMM xo

hearts drawn
in the dark

poems by

R.M. Vaughan

INVISIBLE TO
PREDATORS

ECW PRESS

CANADIAN CATALOGUING IN PUBLICATION DATA

Vaughan, R.M. (Richard Murray), 1965–
Invisible to predators

Poems
ISBN 1-55022-395-X

I. Title.
S8593.A94158 1999   C811'.54   C99-931985-X
PR9199.3.V389I58 1999

Cover and text design by Tania Craan
Cover art: "Monkey on the Chest," Sally McKay, 1996
Author photo by Paul Forsyth
Edited for the press by Michael Holmes
Layout by Mary Bowness
Printed by AGMV l'Imprimeur, Cap-Saint-Ignace, Québec

Distributed in Canada by General Distribution Services,
325 Humber Blvd., Etobicoke, Ontario M9W 7C3

Published by ECW PRESS
2120 Queen Street East, Suite 200,
Toronto, Ontario, M4E 1E2
www.ecw.ca/press

The publication of *Invisible to Predators* has been generously
supported by The Canada Council, the Ontario Arts Council, and
the Government of Canada through the Book Publishing
Industry Development Program.

Contents

Acknowledgements

The author wishes to express his gratitude to The Canada Council For The Arts, The Ontario Arts Council, and The Toronto Arts Council for their financial support.

Poems included in this volume have appeared in the Insomniac Press anthology *Written In The Skin*. "14 Reasons Not To Eat Potato Chips On Church Street" was published as a chapbook by above/ground press. "To Monsieur Desmoulins, dear Camille, in Response to Your Last Letter Before Execution. 206 Years Late." was published as a chapbook by Tortoiseshell & Black Press. Other poems have appeared in the periodicals *The Cormorant*, *The Fiddlehead*, *Navasilu: Journal of English in Sri Lanka*, *Xtra!*, *Rampike*, *Queen Street Quarterly*, *The Gaspereau Review*, *The Church-Wellesley Review*, *POEM*, *Buffet*, *Heavy Girl Press*, *Hook & Ladder*, *The New Brunswick Reader*, *Missing Jacket*, *The James White Review*, *Fascist Panties*, *Wayves Literary Supplement*, *Qwerty*, and *The Link*.

Lost Weekend

a playwaltz, boy to boy   only friends dance so stiffly
the last two stretches of skin left secret between us   tangle and frisk
 — an accident of thighs and American love songs   blurts stories
3 years of conversation never touched on —

a Saturday with tulips and fobbed apologies   both cut at the base
    please, get to the subject (me)   I can understand any kind of love
except foolish delicacy
all mouths accept honey, all eyes take to red petals   hold me, hold me
in your arms and underestimate me

fast dancing, we boys make a near perfect circle, agreeing to its stupidity
to the safety of no partners and hours of drink
 — in another context we're a gang, a frat, the way new inlaws dance and
clap because talking is impossible —
    to notice our cocks all face the empty centre, to notice no boy spins
his backside to his opposite   to notice this is indeed a choreography
marks difference no music drowns

a Tuesday and his rigidity clears the air   shy on the phone, he sings
her body electric and I could kill him because intimacy is like a good
slap   you have to get close to smart and the touch is quick,
noncommittal   fly-blown

forgive me   I thought throwing our bodies together at high speeds
meant something   meant me   in shiftless midmorning, pulling
on a pushed-off shirt, me shitting quietly, me engaged by his bookshelf
because I already read his mind   me, skanky from cum   wanting home

forgive me   I misread his sweat, mistook the press of his fingers
for Morse code   squirreled his spit under the fat of my cheek
like hard candy   took the flag and ran and held out my hand for the next
flash of primary colour and satin to see only air   only my own keys

too early to touch and iron-caked like old pennies   just as useless

I will replay this night over and soon   I'm replaying it now
because I don't believe in perspective or two-headed kings;
there is Courage, and there is not

Men Together

"Nature had taken pains to keep the fatal secret from us. There remains, therefore, only the extraordinary accident of some volcano."

Jean-Jacques Rousseau

acetylene, all manner of racks, pins   the 7 poisons known only to emperors
such ineffective tortures
        to make me talk   My man, just shut up, slam my door   make like the wind
fast and vernal, your voice
    a hard single clink of unnerving airiness
  so brittle — like the skin of firecrackers or seaweed pressed into circles —
  you demand attention   (let it come down, come down)
and I give
peaceful man, keep me up tonight   slap me if you need

pretend it's 1946, and I need bruising, slugging, brandy chasers, a felt hat
knocked to the floor, followed by handshakes
we can be men together   (no one's watching)   we can suffer abrupt
changes of logic, bleary songs at lampposts   midnight prescriptions
(steak over the eye)   because a fire sticks to our skin   leaves
a blackened corn stink, a burnt steam, that smell plugs make after blue sparks
a fire dries our mouths to salt and oily grit, crisped hairs   leaves us
dirty and lonely as puppies

my man, my tired man   light the lights

Gulf

at the small close of skin, the pleat directing balls upward from thighs
grew   an unchecked vertigo and I looked   left, right   seeing only expensive
blankets and double-waxed floors and

           a pitch of open earth beneath me, roaring
with colours I forgot I knew — infatuation yellows, unhealthy   warning
pulses of white, bad news in Orient cultures   enamel red hints, as silly
as nail gloss, as gorgeous — a gulf made brilliant by years sealed from air
from love

spinning, I asked you for water
         (to see if you could step over, to see if you screamed   to see you
piss into the gulch, as any boy might

to watch your feet curl at the cliff side and your shoulders question
the misadventure of crossing)

when you did not say   it's a long walk for water   all was lost

Safe

"Mais, une fois qu'on a commencé de vivre, ca n'en finit plus."
        Anne Hébert, *la robe corail*

yes, I could be transparent, have no more than 2 meanings
for every sentence, smother
my small inhalations in duck-lined beds   (instinctual)
but I am not

            tired, only some part of me, the corner of intellect
reserved for newspapers, educated company, family fights
won't shut up, won't misread for me, play blind man's bluff or
any game with kissing and shut eyes   won't say
— this means nothing, I am safe —

from harm, I take baby steps   dangle limbs over balconies
sit on cane-back chairs made for light men in linens   even dance
fat-legged, convinced of rhythm   but from love   I'm all manner
and logic, knives if necessary   nothing closes me, nothing

to love
no tricks   no practiced feints of hip or cape, no tangles of scarves
to swirl over *the very idea*   because love happened, once, and
like anything charming   love was just another language, another dress,
a sneaky link of party half-grins   spread chair to chair, room to room
    signing the trickster from his mark

Trance

across the room, an enchantment
pulls me by the beltloops   a dropped line
of backbone, kicked up, out to the air
by a high, worked muscle   (his ass)   a lower case
b; mistyped to open a sentence, a novel   long prose
describing several ideas of treasure

after buttons and shirt pockets list, like curtains   a waxed chest
disappoints   so many unnecessary pores and, falling from kisses, no
thatchy corners darker than his face   only skin
aerated and spongy to the fingers

because it counters Nature   this is magic

soon, embarrassed cockrings report   a sudden, tap shoe sound
two thin circles of leather and plastic   one half of illusionist's handcuffs
    neither has truly held me
because Nature is girded, this too is divination

before home, we share fire-orange mugs of hot, sweet tea
— siege hospitality, long after I opened myself —
a drink made for accident victims, rain-beaten protestors, anyone
better off quiet, hands occupied

because my nature is refusing, this is mesmerism

Witness

tonight flesh refuses to be stupid, drape fatly   or not hold red slaps
tonight my witness dock swears in friendly fists — retribution for boring
hours — my cock calls, at the last minute   a surprise witness
veiled in slug-coloured plastic, entering from the back   from the Crown

to the pretty underside   the warm slope hiding veins, white lint,
the little math chains called germs   I apply washes
of colourless spit   hoping for gold under the lead blue, finding
only bruise-red, skin too full with blood for sunlight
hot colours abrasion draws out,
as it will enamels, or the orange at the corner of a tired eye

who made that tattoo eagle in black and green outline, the one clawing its way
to your balls?   a drunk-quick cartoon with 3 legs, a mean joke
a flaw I could live with   for the location
I'm jealous of the needle, the ink   both saw inside you

the truth waits   for a perfect soundstage east light
        his blinds hung bedroom floor to ceiling   cut my left side (the defence desk)
        with broken parallels of morning white   heralding verdicts, the time
to make beds, take seconds to cum, consider sleep in strange linen   walk out
into dawn   matching pink clouds with swollen thighs

razored faces, cleaned for jobs   misjudge the black stubble and off-carmine
compass ringing my mouth   the evidence
gentlemen   I've never been lazy a night in my life

Let It Come Down

we start with spit   wet, clear plastic spun over pinks
3 promises to take time   and jellies
tucked in with fingers   the harder forms of water   (as common,
as untrustworthy)   you can drown in six inches   in seconds

played at fever step, this is not about safety

on mattresses   uneven from use
this is not about fairness   go into me

and miss   appropriate time for a single thread
of white blood   to dash   upstream, a pool waits
                              of the heart but not in it, equally red
relentlessly warm

snow plasma
rest here and grow fat, become rope — silent, sneaky as credit

Tough

squeeze me into a harder ball —
and remember this hide, this leather
        — so unlike the tawny
supplication of days-old bruises, the fat you understand only
because it slinks back to the bone —
                will reflect   and is not for the weak
and you may see yourself, and pace around me   furtive for soft
patches   the way starfish eat sea urchins, from the mouth in

but there's no break in my skin, heartbeats, or negotiations   only
my blood is taken with particles, fractions and counts   steps
invisible to predators

warrior logic: no body has two backs, no castle falls outward

The Needle

to pain, a rude silence   because I won't speak through bust
lips, darting, sugared eyes   or a forehead creased

to pain, a miraculous, stupid courage   it's what's done;
to pain, the sexual miracles visited upon sickrooms in late afternoons

I'm already undressed   any cocked mishap, any Orton farce will do;
to pain let me throw   no waking hours I can spare

the needle, so clean   goes in a dirty place (me) once   and is bent
to a useless and safe L   the orderly's hands cast this new semaphore
for caution — the snapped I, one, index, counting mark, digit, line —
he hardly notices he is making language   (it's the privilege of care-
givers   editing Discomfort's operas to sing-song wheezes and no tears)

he hardly sees my skin closing back on its interruption   to him, my skin
is just a printed surface, a worked quilt   an old poster, pulped
by water and footsteps   because otherwise are tears

Why I Will Not Wear the Red Ribbon at Your Grave

a pride of half-size cars, shrunken from rain, makes squares over green
abused lawn cover
    awful metal gift-boxes stuffed with tricky presents, secret codes
in card form — a generous press of gold, dented fonts spelling
    my faults, my invaded biology — and this attention to parking bylaws,
this courtly hand to glove among drivers   only reminds me that hysteria
while bearing pall, is like human rights in movie houses:
    it is every citizen's privilege to shut up

underfoot, the ground shrugs off our little poems about Circles of Life —
the earth keeps what it takes and I sense   in its little pressures, the aggressive
baby steps back to shape after mucky stumbles
greed   and pleasure   (do not fall, do not give it the Chaplin moment
of down at heart and heels, do not bend)

to say   I know you end here, I know what soil needs   is to announce
madness and doctors are never far from funerals

sleep, kind friends suggest   when the whole problem is closed eyes
and hassock pillows   shiny under waning skin

because the pinpoint of ripe blood widened, heaven opens and
I am not here kissing you, because a violent star
spiny as pollen and smaller   made a nest   I am not discovering the hot
brush hair at the seam of your balls   with my tongue   I mouth thanks
for hotter tea and remember   a paper-cut swipe of plasma made
the white insides between us cherry   beyond bleach   and I cannot run
home and expect your strict hands to tighten me again   so
this, finally, is Family   loose and bloody, easy with death

what we call dirt is really stones, rubbed to atoms, and leftover tangles
of plants, softened by beetles   and forgotten teenage clothes, thrown
from cars   and spit, posters, last summer's charcoal   plus decades of rain

soil is information, bitter to the lips

Berating to Exhale

open up   it's only pudding and blue pills, crushed   on your teeth
a spoon ending in silver flowers, back-heavy   polish it off

you crave the slow down, so quick   a plumb line from mouth to gut
still   as kitchen string on spools or taut behind picture frames or tied
across your abacus   each red bead a bad day, black for good

my math is uneven, but I can read colours   you want to die, like good
governments, in the black

put to bed, your skin under coverlets seeks other whites —
something bone china, a bowl   to push aside, send to earth splintering
but no teddy bears in leather jackets, no ceramic Bachs with lipstick grins
no paintings by anyone under 25 (a sure sign of dying badly) —
you permit only the relentless guilt of lovers
to clutter your room, to sink the foot end of sheets like heavy, restless cats

tuck your tongue up, tip against the dark side of the mouth
one big hand on your jawline, one big hand scissors your nose   look away
neck muscles wire the skin, it is involuntary   (I know this I know you
        do not hate me you are not rethinking)

gulping air the brain fails to miss
your throat hops, a glass ball on a Christmas bough

for an instant we will both see black then, moving off, different lights

excerpts from your diary of this time, in harsh green marker:
I admire chemistry, not mise en scène   either the Wallace Shawn plays
go or I do   I am dying beyond my meaning   touch me, here   yes
again, here   yes, yes

In Camera

you say:

"in this bed tell me a long, hopeless story   to outlast me"

you can forgive your slack thigh fronts, arm muscles undrawn and skin
loose, double toned like velvet   just sitting there
but not throwing over whole days to sleep, not the *in camera* sounds of
two eyeballs cranking under and back just to catch Roman block headlines
or sunlight   in eyes ringed by permanent kohl   then so, so much white
a reverse minstrel

you dislike the pace of your ending, it's like travelling by car   it's hours
before you can stretch, move more than elbows and ankles   no air
between your legs, your only information from an open window

        disease swam between us in red, underground lakes, met
no resistance, no cross tide   because it was only our bodies and geography
doesn't work in inches   so I'll need analogies —
    call this poem a healing ritual and you a shrunken fetish   (bundled with tubing,
blue string from the backs of oxygen masks, fat lengths of chart paper)
    call it last dreams, the way the helpless make worlds

Manifest

things to watch for, mister, when the obituary feels like closure:

the arrival of black flies, uncountable   spelling names of dead
boyfriends on bedroom walls   or broken plates and
green candles burnt clean to the tin X on the bottom, rubbed out
by hoofprints   everywhere, the fogged rank of shit

sure, they're Signs   but so was my note goodbye

I've had too many nights to a novel, to myself   I want fever, not
contemplation   and you ignored that
also at your peril

Seven Good Reasons Why *The Boys In The Band* Could Be A Musical   or, I Am The Dollar In The Dolorosa

(to Cary Fagan)

because in the 4th grade my appendix flew open
    the meat inside, picked out with silver, read: he can only take so much
poison

because the boy whore (from Texas?)   the birthday gift (Act 3)   faced
six red-nosed queens who idled for his love but laughed at his eyes
— a class protected by tight sweaters and memorized cinema, drink mixes
named for riots — laughed because he walked a fat denim knot
at any seated face   and no fag can face such before midnight

because I would be (from Texas?)   and show no care

no   because at 16 Camp is impossible   at 16 you can be scared
or you can be laughing, not both   at 16 a basement bedroom corned
with spunk is a fantasy of loneliness; of tuxedoed, lanky father figures in
late showings of milestone films who must crush you   crying because you
are transparent, and unlucky; of too early peeks
at the shit of a clever life   at 16 you will know panic
so like a bucking gorge, only hotter

because I admit I know nothing of Manhattan rooftops, silvered glass
table lamps, Black men in turtlenecks too swishy for afros or civil rights,
tolerant urban summers cooled with highballs, with Tom Collins,
the suspicious canon of Stonewall, sunken living rooms,
the way cum flakes on orange crushed velvet, like mucilage, generational
gossip about Steve Reeves or Lyle Waggoner, somebody called Cowboy and
everyone laughing, this obsession with "passing"

I cannot be the revisionist bitch powered Marys kick down
the ballroom stairs are closed, there's death in the family

a film ends in a church, and I will mistrust reluctance
in central characters to say I love you   I need better pain than bent
knees, rings of latin poetry, or eyes hot from wick smoke
to say   this is mine, I recognize, this is mine

River Tom

(for Joe Blades)

lakeshore, the sweet clover   white as weddings, taller than me
and men, cottons open at the throat   also white
smell like early honey, honey undigested   not yet wax or combs
lazy before the busy commerce of stinging insects
an honest tang   summer sweet, it marks

the impossibility of hypocrisy at 3 am, in public gardens
dark, civic plains   astounds
our conspiracies of kindnesses, gone with the sun
we see better now, walk with a cat's alacrity

don't misjudge pacing for boredom, we are
genuine killers, unable to sleep   (the knives   the knives   )
                circling dogwoods, finished lilacs, blown milkweed
displacing evidential dust for Love

Tonight, I remember Hermann Goering's last best friend
— the American prison guard, fascinated by iron or
a general dull gleam, missing the simple evil of his American
oceans — and we decide, like him,
to slip, because falling is attractive
to make pals with our daylight devils   decide
to fuck what frightens

is this a method of whispering?   your tongue, warm
as tap water, snubbed at the end   a wet fish head
sorel-red   fitting uneasily, slippery over
the raised grades of my ear
                you want to tell me something
    dark and lovely
perhaps forget my name   (I lied anyway)   or turn on me
the moray in the pink coral, biting

because you're scared

oh, my sweet purchase   a kiss?   thunder, barbed
leaves or salt under the clouds hardly
prevent our heat

touch me, the city can't afford searchlights   never bothers
with bloodhounds   for 2 shirtless boys
thick as outdoor leather   caught in the low candelabra of alders
a Puck, an Ariel
for the muck, the rime   later, worms

Vanity Fare

(for Lynn Crosbie)

because at 1 pm no one deserves a proper breakfast

tapwater and pillbox are toast and eggs

      daybreak in two swallows

in haste

my lips pop open, mimic koi in warm water   drop

between the tin crosshairs   (designed to stop diamonds or eyebrow pencils

                                    sometimes tears)

            the orange disc of secret proteins, my tiny shield

and I wail   because without that dollhouse cake, that morning tourniquet

                chemistry's helpful star

all my air and light   maybe bravery

  slinks to the underhouse beneath the taps

                      the dark land

           veined with lead, links of green copper and pink clays

  goes to fishes

or worse   under the knowing noon and eyes

            of cashiers and doctors   people used to liars

          I make dramatic, red silk at my neck and leathered fingers

        covering bloody indexes hard done

      by metal traps   by the scraggy cut of tin by

waking up ugly and afraid by a dirty sink

"There is a power at work, enticing everything to dance to a single rhythm. Nobody knows what suffering this causes —"

Naguib Mahfouz, *The Harafish*

(for Michael Holmes)

tears across the telephone, why is no one shocked?
electrically, hugging on College St.   my face angled for kisses

of chocolate & coconut & other European compromises   we match stories
told to a panhandler, any Friday night: I dislike folk music

for the gods   for the gods   for the gods   3 palaces
along Davenport, you promise to take me in should I go mad

Lee, a Montreal poet in unwise leotards   crowds the backseat sexually
undone   and the book reviews, undone   plus poems

by anyone, anyone not Canadian   I could stand, forgetting to wilt
my cock (in half force) says   tonight is only an hour from over

cloud covers, yet under a blue so rigid   flight must frighten birds
remember any free meal — keep a diary, a budget of handouts   you're an artist

my raconteur, gorgeous   defeats fibre optics (what translation for tears?)
in the cloth of nightsky, hold me against meteors   sharp bits of stars

Simone Signoret, Beldam

(for Peter Lynch)

under water, her limed hands spread   the basest ligature, each
    delects in murder and, later, another butter-white cigarette (*tabac*
Maroc, on the eve of Franz Fanon)   glints, a bright
contrary to the sneaky, fattening purples of Klieg lights, the illegal
lead in post-war cold creams   the off-colour flush of the play murderess

you watch, think   it can't be so easy
to put a life out under the tap   to make her woman's hands grave as rocks
as oars   to disregard the exigency of Plot

harsh and distracted, she is confident of more grey suits, more tiled
floors clicking dykish impatience   more pleated fronts and wet grass
to buff the heat between her breasts   a hundred more movies
fixated with bathtubs

later, she will publish, speak out, resist a government, bed Palestinians
(or was that Françoise Sagan?)   forget her lines, drink at breakfast
finally   snap — as only a living argument can — behind a parked
Mustang, vomiting before her 200th public defence of the auteur theory
    the hateful siren charge of patricide

Celebrity is a ticklish fabric

Rimbaud:
    "That is all in the past. Nowadays I know how to greet beauty."

backwards Ophelia, citizeness

The Follies, Alexander Street

"I wondered irrelevantly if I was to be caught with a teapot in my hand on every dramatic occasion?"

      Barbara Pym

In the pine-soaped tingle of lobby air, I take his hand
and agree to be less of a man
I'm like that   it's my posture   (Oh) embraceable me
I'm spined like a cat, ass hitched for sunshine
Lust's little buddy   a rash of kisses follows

This is what I expect from sex with my elders:
impatience, a fear of violent bed noises
baby words for cocks (wiener, bird)
and incest metaphors   also
the flat ginger taste of bath powder on his balls or other flags
of racing femininity
        he's planning for his incapacity, twenty years ahead
I'm looking for Daddy   the rest is script:
        palm on my red shoulder, he's jumpy with cum   he's boyish and revived
            (Higher! Papa! Higher!)
        he imagines another good hour of rough tricks
but changes his mind   sleeping off what he already lost
              (Lie still, Father   dream of railed beds & nighty-nights
from nurses   then the oak box)

On his terrace I drink warm Pepsi, wonder at trees changing and a summer
plundered, the Prime Minister's madness, recent murders   (banalities all)

because I called him Daddy and accepted slaps

and we stopped   3 wails before tears

and I called him Daddy   after salty hugs   and in his kitchen

the radio is playing a giggling samba beat and I'm ridiculous

because I called him Daddy, and it could have been true

The McHugh Suite

foyer

rub the ends of my fingers   it is starting to be November   now stop
before dinner any undressed friction has consequences
(there is so much food in this house
you put a poor boy to shame)   it says — sneak a right hand under
his belt, dart your half-angry cock expertly
be safe as keys in pockets — then wait
till so, so much talking later   with linen napkins, white jazz   and no
arguments   I'm just in the door

kitchen

5 wine-red truth-tellings he spilled on bone-white lozenge tile
any sensible faggot would understand to be warnings:

looking forward to Christmas
fear of big dogs
the phrase "benefit of the doubt"
my alcoholism, handled like parchment   the Magna Carta
wiping, wiping   every crumb and spot met with damp cloth   hand towels
by the bed

I shoulda ran, remembered Jimmy Stewart in *Vertigo*   doubles

chasing doubles, too many grey twin sets on blondes
shoulda seen the bell tower only leads down after up
lateral is a luxury (and I have so few, I guard myself   no
        I never do)

library

because the blushing stopped with kisses
(and nerve ends at lips like to be bitten, like to swell
feel sour and rough   as if facing winter gusts
only to wet, in instants   on chins or the roots of necks)
I trust you enough, throw my tongue across your incisors
past the tiny saws   meeting the dull, heavy molars   with grace

you cut the blue hamstrings   take the meat
fat and bloody in your cheek   walk away, spit the hot triangle
of exposed muscle down the sink   rinse with orange and gin
change shirts, worry about bleach vs. protein   reflect
on the ease of a boyfriend who only nods or shakes
prefers books to talk

living room

touched by the generosity and muscle of my limbs
you pull the four points of my starred body   handhandfootfoot
over you, over your duck-stuffed sofa
my extremities — fixed contrary to the line the couch marks
between comforts — pinwheel   from dining (left hand) to living (right
hand) to reading (left foot) to making love (right foot)

little me   I'm highlighting your interiors, I'm an asterik
I'm compassing your terrain   I'm being a Top —
and now you don't like that

Manufactured by Amazon.ca
Bolton, ON

10722491R10068